As Mia watched the bird, all sounds of traffic went away. The sun was still shining, but the light seemed to change. The sky was different. It's like looking at an old photograph, she thought. An old, brown photograph. What's happening?

Mia is on holiday by the sea, in Crytchmoor. It's a small, quiet place, with the usual beaches, the usual shops, the usual people . . .

But this is going to be the most *un*usual holiday Mia will ever have. There is the mystery of the beach at Crytch Cove – the beach that no one will go near. There is Jake, the strange boy who knows things that he will not talk about. And then there is the bird . . .

The bird that she sees everywhere, that seems to watch her – and seems to want to *take* her somewhere . . . somewhere in *time*!

John Escott has written many books for readers of all ages. Many of these are mystery or detective stories.

He was born in a small town in Somerset, in the west of England, and worked in business before he started to write books. He now lives with his wife in Bournemouth, Dorset, by the sea, and has two children and two grandchildren. When he is not writing, he likes walking along empty beaches and watching the sea near his home.

Other Penguin Readers by John Escott are *The Ghost of Genny Castle*, *Money to Burn* and *Detective Work*.

The following titles are available at Levels 2, 3 and 4:

Level 2
The Birds
The Canterville Ghost and the Model
  Millionaire
Chocky
The Diary
Don't Look Behind You
Don't Look Now
Emily
Flour Babies
The Fox
The Ghost of Genny Castle
Grandad's Eleven
The Lady in the Lake
Money to Burn
Persuasion
The Railway Children
The Room in the Tower and Other
  Ghost Stories
Simply Suspense
Treasure Island
Under the Greenwood Tree
The Wave
We Are All Guilty
The Weirdo

Level 3
Black Beauty
The Black Cat and Other Stories
The Book of Heroic Failures
Braveheart
Calling All Monsters
A Catskill Eagle
Channel Runner
The Darling Buds of May
Dubliners
Earthdark
Forrest Gump
The Fugitive
Jane Eyre
King Solomon's Mines

Madame Doubtfire
The Man with Two Shadows and
  Other Ghost Stories
More Heroic Failures
Mrs Dalloway
My Family and Other Animals
Not a Penny More, Not a Penny Less
Rain Man
The Reluctant Queen
Santorini
Sherlock Holmes and the Mystery
  of Boscombe Pool
StarGate
Summer of My German Soldier
The Thirty-nine Steps
Thunder Point
The Turn of the Screw
Twice Shy

Level 4
The Boys from Brazil
The Breathing Method
The Burden of Proof
The Client
The Danger
Detective Work
The Doll's House and Other Stories
Dracula
Far from the Madding Crowd
Farewell, My Lovely
Glitz
Gone with the Wind, Part 1
Gone with the Wind, Part 2
The House of Stairs
The Locked Room and Other
  Horror Stories
The Mill on the Floss
The Mosquito Coast
The Picture of Dorian Gray
Strangers on a Train
White Fang

For a complete list of the titles available in the Penguin Readers series please write to the following address for a catalogue: Penguin ELT Marketing Department, Penguin Books Ltd, 27 Wrights Lane, London W8 5TZ.

Time Bird

JOHN ESCOTT

Level 3

Series Editor: Derek Strange

PENGUIN BOOKS

PENGUIN BOOKS

Published by the Penguin Group
Penguin Books Ltd, 27 Wrights Lane, London W8 5TZ, England
Penguin Books USA Inc., 375 Hudson Street, New York, New York 10014, USA
Penguin Books Australia Ltd, Ringwood, Victoria, Australia
Penguin Books Canada Ltd, 10 Alcorn Avenue, Toronto, Ontario, Canada M4V 3B2
Penguin Books (NZ) Ltd, 182–190 Wairau Road, Auckland 10, New Zealand

Penguin Books Ltd, Registered Offices: Harmondsworth, Middlesex, England

First published by Penguin Books 1993
3 5 7 9 10 8 6 4 2

Text copyright © John Escott 1993
Illustrations copyright © Bob Harvey (Pennant Illustrators) 1993
All rights reserved

The moral right of the author and of the illustrator has been asserted

Typeset by Datix International Limited, Bungay, Suffolk
Set in 12/14 pt Lasercomp Bembo
Printed in England by Clays Ltd, St Ives plc

To the teacher:

In addition to all the language forms of Levels One and Two, which are used again at this level of the series, the main verb forms and tenses used at Level Three are:

- past continuous verbs, present perfect simple verbs, conditional clauses (using the 'first' or 'open future' conditional), question tags and further common phrasal verbs
- modal verbs: *have (got) to* and *don't have to* (to express obligation), *need to* and *needn't* (to express necessity), *could* and *was able to* (to describe past ability), *could* and *would* (in offers and polite requests for help), and *shall* (for future plans, offers and suggestions).

Also used are:
- relative pronouns: *who*, *that* and *which* (in defining clauses)
- conjunctions: *if* and *since* (for time or reason), *so that* (for purpose or result) and *while*
- indirect speech (questions)
- participle clauses.

Specific attention is paid to vocabulary development in the Vocabulary Work exercises at the end of the book. These exercises are aimed at training students to enlarge their vocabulary systematically through intelligent reading and effective use of a dictionary.

To the student:

Dictionary Words:
- When you read this book, you will find that some words are darker black than the others on the page. Look them up in your dictionary, if you do not already know them, or try to guess the meaning of the words first, without a dictionary.

Before you read:

Look at the picture and answer the questions below.

1 Where do you think these people are?
2 Why do you think they are here? To work? To have a holiday?
3 What time of year do you think it is? Summer or winter?
4 Look at the name of the story. What does it tell you about the story you are going to read?
5 Which of the following things can you see in the picture?
   a boat   a bird   a dog   a suitcase   an aeroplane

Chapter One

FIG COTTAGE

Mia saw the **advertisement** in the newspaper.

Do you need a holiday? Stay at our low-cost holiday **cottage**. Write to Mrs Gurney, Elm House, Sea Road, Crytchmoor. Telephone number: Crytchmoor 517383.

'We do need a holiday,' said Mia.

Mrs Dilon didn't like holidays. 'I can't leave the office at the moment,' she said. 'We're very busy.'

'You need a rest,' Grandpa Morgan told her. 'You'll work better after a holiday.'

Mrs Dilon didn't answer for a minute. She looked at her father and her daughter. 'Perhaps you're right,' she said. 'But I can only take a few days.'

'I'll phone Mrs Gurney now,' said Mia, smiling.

◆

Two weeks later, a bird flew silently over Fig Cottage and landed on the roof. Below, a car stopped outside the cottage and three people got out. The bird watched them. A woman, an older man, and a girl fifteen years old. They took bags and suitcases from the car, and then looked at the cottage.

'It will be better inside,' said Grandpa Morgan.

'I hope so,' said Mrs Dilon.

'It's OK,' Mia told her mother. 'We're only here for a few days.'

She looked round. The cottage was on the **cliff** top, a few metres from the road. There were no other cottages or houses near it. At the bottom of the cliff was a beach and the sea. Mia looked for a **path** to the beach. There was one, but there was a **sign** at the top of the path. It said: DANGER. KEEP OUT.

'How can we get down to Crytch Cove beach?' Mia wanted to know.

'Perhaps there's another path,' said Grandpa Morgan.

Crytch Cove was three kilometres from the small town of Crytchmoor.

'There was a nice beach at Crytchmoor,' said Mrs Dilon. 'I saw it when we came through in the car. We can use that instead of Crytch Cove. It's not far to go.'

She and Grandpa Morgan moved towards the cottage. Mia picked up her suitcase ready to follow them.

The bird flew off the roof.

Mia looked up and saw it. A **herring gull**, she thought.

Then something strange happened. She suddenly felt odd. How did she feel? She didn't know.

◆

As Mia watched the bird, all sounds of traffic went away. The sun was still shining, but the light seemed to change. The sky was different. It's like looking at an old photograph, she thought. An old, brown photograph. What's happening?

'Come on, Mia,' said Mrs Dilon. 'What are you looking at?'

'That bird,' answered Mia. 'The herring gull.'

Mrs Dilon looked up at the sky. 'Bird? What bird?' She looked at Mia strangely and went inside.

The bird is there, thought Mia. I'm watching it!
But then it disappeared.

◆

Mia closed her eyes and opened them again. The traffic noises returned, the light changed back. It was an ordinary sunny day again.

She walked into the cottage with her suitcase. Did I see the herring gull? she thought. Or did I dream it?

◆

It seemed dark inside the cottage. There were two rooms downstairs, and one was a kitchen. Mia looked out of the window and saw a garden. Some grass, a few flowers and a wooden **fence**. The other room in the cottage was bigger. The furniture in it was old and heavy. Mia sat in a big leather armchair.

'I'll make some tea,' said Mrs Dilon, going into the kitchen.

Grandpa Morgan sat in a chair by a large round table. He smiled at Mia. 'Your mother will like it after a day or two,' he said. 'She needs a rest from her work. This holiday was a good idea.'

There was a knock at the door.

'I'll answer it,' said Mia.

She opened the door and saw a man standing outside. He was tall and thin and his hair was going grey.

'Hallo,' he said. 'I'm Jack Gurney. My wife asked me to come and make sure that you have everything you need.'

'Come in,' said Mia. 'Mum's making some tea. Will you have some?'

Jack Gurney smiled. 'Thanks,' he said.

9

*Mia watched him. Something's wrong, she thought. Something
he isn't telling us . . .*

The tall man came into the cottage, and Mia told her
mother and grandfather who he was.

Mrs Dilon gave him a cup of tea. 'We seem to have
everything we want,' she said. 'The cottage is old, isn't it?'

'Yes, it is,' said Jack Gurney. 'When we came to Crytchmoor in 1968, we lived here. Then we decided to buy a
house in the town, and to make Fig Cottage a holiday cottage.'

'Where's the path down to the beach at Crytch Cove?'
asked Mia. 'There's a DANGER sign at the top of the path
across the road.'

Jack Gurney drank some of his tea. He didn't look at
Mia when he answered her. 'Not many people go down to

Crytch Cove beach,' he said. 'There's a path, about two kilometres along the cliff road. But there's a nicer beach at Crytchmoor. You go there, it's not far away.'

Mia watched him. Something's wrong, she thought. Something he isn't telling us. He doesn't want us to go to Crytch Cove. Why?

Chapter Two

THE BOY FROM THE FAIR

After Jack Gurney had gone, Mia went up to her bedroom. It was a small room with a bed under the window. Mia climbed over the bed to look across the fields at the back of Fig Cottage.

There was a **fair** in one of the fields. She saw the Big Wheel moving round, and heard sounds of far-away music. Mia smiled. She liked fairs. She liked to ride on the **merry-go-round**, to go up into the sky on the Big Wheel.

Perhaps we can go to the fair one evening, she thought. Fairs are more exciting at night. I like the bright coloured lights, and the loud music.

She took her clothes out of her suitcase. The weather will be hot and sunny, she thought, and we'll have a good holiday.

Grandpa Morgan and Mrs Dilon wanted to sit in the garden that afternoon. 'I was driving for nearly five hours this morning,' said Mia's mother. 'I think I'll sit in the sun until this evening.'

'That's a good idea,' said Grandpa Morgan. He found some garden chairs in the kitchen, and carried them out into the garden.

'I'm going to walk along the cliff top,' said Mia. 'I'll take my **binoculars** and watch the birds.'

'Keep away from the path to the Cove,' warned Mrs Dilon. 'It's dangerous.'

The sun was hot on Mia's head as she walked. I need a sun hat, she thought. Perhaps I'll get one tomorrow.

She looked out at the sea through her binoculars. There was a large red and blue boat sailing across the water. It was full of people. Mia watched them through her binoculars. They were walking up and down the boat, looking out at the sea. She could see them drinking from tins of Coca Cola and eating ice-cream.

I'll have a ride on that boat tomorrow, thought Mia. I like going on the sea.

She moved her binoculars and looked along the cliffs. She was able to see down to Crytch Cove beach, but there were no people on it.

Jack Gurney was right, thought Mia. People don't seem to go to Crytch Cove. How strange. She looked along the side of the cliff at the birds. Mia loved to watch birds. Sometimes I think they can do magic things, she thought. How do they know when to fly to warm countries in the winter? How can they find their way back again? That's a sort of magic.

Most of the cliff side was covered with grass, but on one part there was only a large flat **rock**. What was there? thought Mia. Why is there no grass on that part? It seems odd.

A boy was walking along the top of the cliff towards her. He looked the same age as Mia. He was wearing jeans and a T-shirt, and his hair was thick and black.

'Hi,' he said. 'Are you on holiday?'

A boy was walking along the top of the cliff towards Mia. He looked the same age as her.

'Yes,' replied Mia. 'We arrived this afternoon. Are you on holiday, too?'

'I'm with the fair,' the boy said. 'My Dad works on the big merry-go-round.' He looked down at Crytch Cove. 'We come every year at this time. I hate it. It's better in Crytchmoor. This place . . .' He stopped.

'Go on,' said Mia. 'What's wrong with this place? Nobody seems to like it.'

'It's not a happy place,' he said. 'I don't know – it's difficult to explain.'

'Have you been down to the beach at Crytch Cove?' asked Mia.

'Yes,' he said. 'It's not a nice place. I feel uncomfortable when I'm down there.'

'Why?' said Mia.

'I don't know,' he answered. He looked across at Fig Cottage. 'Are you staying there?'

'Yes,' Mia told him. 'My mother and grandfather are with me.' He still didn't look happy, Mia noticed. 'Is there something wrong with the cottage?' she asked.

'Other young people have stayed there,' he said. 'Some strange things happened to them.'

'What strange things?' asked Mia.

The boy didn't answer. He began to walk away, then he looked back. 'My name is Jake,' he said. 'What's yours?'

'Mia,' she told him.

He smiled. 'See you, Mia.' And he ran off towards the fair.

◆

Mia went up to her bedroom when she got back to the cottage. She wanted to read a book until it was time to eat, and she decided to stay in her room.

But as soon as Mia began to read, she started to think about Jake. *What did he mean about the other young people staying at the cottage?* she thought. *What strange things happened to them when they were here? And why does nobody go to Crytch Cove beach?*

It was all a mystery. But the long drive from home and the walk along the top of the cliff was making her sleepy. Mia closed her eyes.

She dreamed about the bird, the herring gull on the roof. In her dream, Mia was following the bird down a path and through tall grass. She was running, but her feet didn't seem to be touching the ground at all. Suddenly, she was falling . . . falling . . . Mia screamed . . .

And then she was awake.

She could hear the sound of her heart, and she was shaking. It was only a dream, she told herself.

She sat up on the bed and looked out of the window. Outside the sun was still shining. She looked across the fields at the back of Fig Cottage. Looked for the fair . . .

. . . *But there was no fair. The fields were empty. Once again, the light was different. It was like looking at an old brown photograph again. The sun lost its brightness, the grass was not so green.*

*Mia looked across at the cliff road. There were no cars or buses. But there were two black lines above the road. They're like **trolley** bus lines, she thought. I've seen pictures of trolley buses in books. Were the lines there when I walked along the top of the cliff? I'm sure they weren't.*

And then Mia saw the bird, flying across the sky. The black and grey herring gull. She was sure it was the same one. She

There were two black lines above the road. They're like trolley bus lines, Mia thought.

watched until it disappeared. Then she looked back across the fields . . .

. . . And there was the fair again. The Big Wheel, the merry-go-round, the sound of music.

Mia looked back at the cliff road.

The black lines were gone.

Chapter Three

THE MYSTERY OF CRYTCH COVE

The next morning, they went into Crytchmoor. Mia took her binoculars and a camera with her. It was ten o'clock and already the day was very hot.

'We need sun hats,' said Mrs Dilon.

There were some shops near the beach and they went to look in them. They stopped outside a little shop which sold newspapers, postcards, sun glasses and sun hats.

'I like that one,' said Mia, pointing at a sun hat with gulls painted on it.

Mrs Dilon laughed. 'That's because it has birds on it,' she said. 'You and your birds!'

Mia laughed with her. They each bought a hat and then went down to the beach. There were a lot of people there, some swimming in the sea and others sitting in **deck-chairs**.

Mia put on her swimsuit and ran down to the water. She was a good swimmer and it was warm in the water. She saw the red and blue boat again. It was ready to sail and people were getting on to it.

I'll do that later, thought Mia. I like a boat trip.

After they finished eating their lunch on the beach, Mia went off to the boat. She took her camera and her binoculars with her. Her sun hat kept the hot sun off her head, and she bought a ticket and found a place on the boat.

The boat went out to a little island near Crytchmoor. It sailed round the island, then came back along the coast. Mia watched the other, smaller boats on the sea. She looked through her binoculars at the birds flying above them.

Then she turned and looked at the cliff when the boat sailed in front of Crytch Cove. Again, she saw the large flat rock where there was no grass.

Did something happen there? she thought.

Other people were looking at Crytch Cove and its empty beach. Two women were talking near Mia and she heard some of the things they were saying.

'. . . I was only a child then,' said one. She was wearing a yellow dress and large sun glasses. 'It was terrible.'

'People don't want to remember,' said the other woman. 'And nobody likes to use the beach any more.'

The two women moved away.

What were they talking about? thought Mia. What is it people don't want to remember?

After her boat trip, Mia went for a walk through the town. The streets were narrow and the little shops were full of tourists. Mia stopped at a small café and bought a cold drink.

She thought about the women on the boat, and about Jake and Mr Gurney. She was sure something happened at Crytch Cove, probably a long time ago. What did the

Mia bought a ticket and found a place on the boat. The boat went out to a little island near Crytchmoor.

woman say? *I was only a child then.* And now nobody liked going to the cove. Mr Gurney didn't like it, and neither did Jake. Why?

She looked over the road and saw a shop selling old books and postcards. After she had finished her drink, Mia went across. The shopkeeper was sitting in a deckchair outside. He was reading a book, but looked up and smiled at Mia.

'Can I help you?' he asked.

'I just want to look round,' said Mia.

'Please do,' said the shopkeeper.

There was a table outside the shop window. It was covered with books and boxes of old postcards. Mia started to look through the postcards.

Most of them were old pictures of Crytchmoor. She found one with a picture of the cliff road, and noticed something.

Trolley bus lines went all the way along the cliff road.

'There *were* trolley buses here!' she said to herself.

The shopkeeper heard her and looked up from his book. 'Trolley buses?' he said. 'Yes, there were trolley buses in Crytchmoor, a long time ago. They were nice quiet things.'

'How long ago did they stop?' asked Mia.

The man thought for a minute. '1958, I think,' he said.

Mia walked back to the beach. Why did I see trolley bus lines through my bedroom window? she thought. *Did* I see them? Or did I dream them?

But Mia knew it was not a dream.

Later, when they were back at Fig Cottage having a meal, Mia asked her mother a question.

'Do you think it's possible to see into the past?' she said.

There was a table outside the shop window. It was covered with books and boxes of old postcards.

'To see something that was there a long time ago, but not now.'

Her mother looked at her strangely. 'What an odd question,' she said. 'No, it's not possible.'

Grandpa Morgan drank some coffee, then said, 'How do we know? How do we know that the past, now, and the future isn't all happening together? Perhaps we can go from one time to another time.'

'How? With a Time Machine?' said Mia.

'Or with somebody, some*thing* to show us the way,' said Grandpa Morgan.

Mia looked out of the window. She was thinking about the herring gull.

Chapter Four

THE MERRY-GO-ROUND

That evening, Mia and Grandpa Morgan went over the fields to the fair. The coloured lights on the Big Wheel moved in a circle in front of the dark sky. The music was loud and happy, and Mia forgot about ghostly herring gulls and trolley bus lines that were not there.

They had a ride on the big merry-go-round. Mia sat on the back of a brightly coloured wooden horse and looked for Jake, but did not see him. The man working on the merry-go-round looked a bit like Jake.

That's Jake's father, thought Mia.

After the merry-go-round ride, Mia went on the Big Wheel alone. Sitting high up in the sky, Mia saw Fig Cottage. She saw the light in the window downstairs. It's a

*When Mia came down off the Big Wheel, she saw Jake
near the merry-go-round. 'Hi!' she shouted.*

nice cottage, she thought, but strange things do happen there.

When she came down off the Big Wheel, she saw Jake near the merry-go-round. 'Hi!' she shouted.

He looked round. 'Oh, hallo,' he said, coming across.

'This is Jake,' Mia explained to her grandfather. 'I'm glad I've seen you,' she told Jake, when Grandpa Morgan went to get some drinks for them. 'I wanted to ask you about the other children.'

'What other children?' said Jake.

'The children who have stayed at Fig Cottage,' said Mia. 'What happened to them? Did they – did they see things? Things that weren't really there?'

Jake didn't answer for a minute. Then he said, 'Why?'

'Because I think I've seen things that aren't really there,' said Mia.

'What did you see?' Jake asked quickly.

'Trolley bus lines,' said Mia. 'But the trolley buses stopped years ago.'

'What other things have you seen?' asked Jake.

'Yesterday, I couldn't see the fair – and then I could,' said Mia. 'It went away, then it came back.'

Jake was silent for another minute, then he said, 'Have you seen . . . a bird?'

'Oh, yes, the herring gull!' said Mia. She looked at him. '*You've* seen it, haven't you? What does it mean?'

There was a frightened look in Jake's eyes. 'I don't know,' he said.

And he ran off towards the merry-go-round.

Grandpa Morgan came back with the drinks. 'What happened to Jake?' he asked.

'He – he had to help his Dad,' said Mia.

That night, Mia's dreams were full of painted animals. Animals on a merry-go-round. Then there were faces. Faces of frightened people – young men, women, children – going round and round on the merry-go-round.

Suddenly, people began to scream. But the screams coming from their mouths were the KYOW! KYOW! noises of herring gulls . . .

Mia woke up, crying. She did not go back to sleep again.

♦

Next morning, Grandpa Morgan was feeling ill.

'I had a bit too much sun yesterday, I think,' he said. 'I'll go back to bed for an hour. You two go on down to the beach.'

'I have some shopping to do first,' said Mrs Dilon. 'Do you want to come with me, Mia?'

Mia hated shopping. 'No, thanks,' she said. 'I think I'll sit in the garden and read my book.'

So Grandpa Morgan went back to bed and Mrs Dilon drove off to Crytchmoor in the car. Mia got her book and sun hat from the bedroom, then sat in the garden.

It was hot and quiet there. Mia heard the sound of a gull now and then. Not the herring gull, she noticed, just ordinary gulls. She read some of her book, but her night without much sleep was making her feel tired. She closed her eyes and put her head back on the grass. The book dropped on to the ground next to her.

She was almost asleep when the bird began to make its noise.

KYOW! KYOW!

'Herring gull,' Mia said, opening her eyes.

The bird was in front of her.

'You!' she said. She watched it for a minute. 'I'm going to call you Fig because you seem to belong to this cottage.'

The bird stood on the grass. It had a white front, a yellow **beak**, and grey **wings**. Suddenly, it flew away. Mia noticed that it made no sound when it flew. It did not go far, only to the fence at the end of the garden. Then it turned and looked back at her.

'What do you want, Fig?' said Mia. 'Are you asking me to follow you? I can't *fly*.' But she stood up and walked over to the fence.

The bird flew on, across the cliff road. Then on towards the path that went down to the beach. It dropped into the high grass and **bushes**.

Mia waited to see the bird fly up again, but nothing happened. Was the herring gull hurt? She went to the end of the garden and climbed on to the fence . . .

. . . *And a strange feeling came over her. There was a sound in her ears – a loud* KYOW! KYOW! *But she could not see the bird. And the light was different. It was like looking at an old brown photograph again. The sun was not bright, but it was still there.*

Mia jumped down from the fence and ran across the road. There were the black trolley bus lines again. And the road was rough under her feet. She ran on to the top of the cliff, and there was the path in front of her.

There was no DANGER *sign. The grass was short and tidy, and so were the bushes. Mia went down the path. Something – someone – seemed to be pulling her along.*

'Fig!' she shouted.

The bird answered with a KYOW! *but she could not see it. On*

Mia went, down the path. Down and down. She went past people who were walking in front of her. Their clothes looked strange.

They are clothes from years ago, not clothes of today, Mia thought.

The sun was not bright but it was hot. Mia looked up and saw the herring gull in the sky. It was flying towards the sea.

She went past two small children with their mother. The children looked at her strangely and began to laugh. They were pointing at Mia's clothes. They think my clothes are odd, she thought.

The path went round a corner and Mia followed it. And there in front of her was Crytch Cove beach . . .

But it was not empty like the beach Mia saw from the boat. There were crowds of people all over it. Children making **castles** in the **sand**. People sitting in deckchairs or swimming in the sea.

At the back of the beach was a merry-go-round. Children and young people were riding on wooden animals, and the animals had painted faces.

Mia watched them going round.

It's like my dream! she thought.

She closed her eyes. What was happening to her?

Suddenly, there was a voice coming from somewhere.

'Mia?' The voice seemed to come from far away . . .

. . . Mia opened her eyes and looked behind her. She saw her mother coming down the path towards her.

'What are you doing?' her mother was saying. 'Why did you come down here, Mia? It's dangerous!'

Mia looked back at the beach. She looked for the children

27

The path went round a corner and Mia followed it. And there in front of Mia was Crytch Cove beach . . .

making castles in the sand. She looked for the people sitting in deckchairs or swimming in the sea.

But there was nobody there.

Chapter Five

ACCIDENT

'I didn't know where you were,' Mrs Dilon told Mia. 'I was worried.'

They were eating their lunch in the cottage. Grandpa Morgan was still resting in bed.

Shall I tell her about Fig? thought Mia. Will she believe me? She put down her knife and fork. 'I followed a bird,' she said.

'How stupid!' said Mrs Dilon. She was angry.

Mia decided to say no more.

That afternoon, Mia and her mother went to Crytchmoor. Mrs Dilon took a book to read on the beach. Mia went into the town to buy some postcards to send to her friends at home.

She was coming out of a shop when she saw Jake. He was crossing the road. He saw her and waved.

'I've just bought some postcards,' she told him when he came over. 'What are you doing?'

'Just looking round,' he said.

'Come and have a cup of coffee,' said Mia. 'I've got something to tell you.'

Jake looked surprised but followed her to the café. It was the café opposite the book shop, and they sat at a table outside. A waitress brought them two coffees.

*They sat at a table outside the café. A waitress brought them
two coffees.*

'What do you want to tell me?' asked Jake.

'I saw the herring gull today,' she said.

'Did you?' he said.

'I followed it down to Crytch Cove,' Mia told him. 'But it wasn't . . . *today* when I got down there. Do you understand?'

Jake did not answer for a minute. Then he said, 'Yes, I understand. It happened to me, last year. I followed the herring gull down to the beach.'

'What did you see?' asked Mia.

'People,' he said.

'And a merry-go-round?' she asked.

'I can't remember,' he said. 'I didn't go on to the sand.'

'How did you know it wasn't today?' said Mia. 'How did you know it was a long time ago?'

'Because the people were wearing strange clothes,' said Jake. 'The sort you see in old photographs.'

'Yes, I noticed that,' said Mia. She looked across the road at the book shop. 'Finish your coffee,' she told Jake. 'We're going to look at some old photographs.'

The shopkeeper was sitting outside the shop again. He looked surprised to see Mia.

'I want to show my friend the postcards,' said Mia.

'Please, do,' said the shopkeeper.

They went through the boxes of postcards but Mia couldn't find the one she wanted.

'What are you looking for?' asked the shopkeeper.

'Pictures of Crytch Cove,' said Mia. 'Crytch Cove a long time ago.'

'Before the accident?' asked the shopkeeper.

Mia and Jake looked at him. 'What accident?' they said together.

The man got up from his chair and they followed him into the shop. He took a book from a table and opened it.

'It happened on the 8th of August, 1956,' the shopkeeper said. He pointed to a picture in the book. Mia and Jake looked at it.

It was an old photograph of Crytch Cove. There was something wrong with part of the cliff, Mia noticed.

'What happened?' she asked.

'They were building a house,' said the shopkeeper. 'It belonged to a rich man who lived in Crytchmoor. He wanted a new house on the side of the cliff, with a swimming pool and a beautiful garden. But something went wrong when they were building it. Part of the cliff fell down. It fell on to the beach below –'

'On to the merry-go-round on the beach!' said Mia. 'That's why the people were screaming!'

'What people?' said Jake.

'The people in my dream!' said Mia.

The shopkeeper looked at her strangely, then went on speaking. 'The beach was closed for the rest of that summer,' he said. 'Nobody wanted to go there after the accident. They still don't want to go there. It is not a good place any more. Perhaps there are ghosts . . .'

'What happened to the house on the cliff?' asked Jake.

'It was pulled down,' said the shopkeeper. 'The man didn't want to live there after the accident. It's strange, but there's no grass on that part of the cliff. There's only a big flat rock where they were building the house.'

'I've seen it,' said Mia.

The shopkeeper turned more pages in the book. He pointed to another picture of Crytch Cove. 'A photographer took this picture for the 1957 Crytchmoor Tourist Guide Book, only minutes before the accident,' he said. 'But he didn't use it.'

Mia looked at the people in the photograph. Happy people on holiday. The merry-go-round was at the back of the beach, under the cliff. She remembered the people on the 'long-ago' beach she saw that morning. She remembered the 'different' clothes. *They were the same as the clothes in the picture*.

A woman came into the shop and waved to the shop-keeper. The man gave Mia the book and went across to the woman.

'Can I help you?' he said.

Mia turned the pages of the book. 'You and I both saw the Cove before the accident,' she said to Jake. 'How long before? A few hours? A few minutes?'

'I don't know,' said Jake. He seemed uncomfortable. 'Let's go.'

'In a minute,' Mia said. She was looking at a picture of a trolley bus going along the cliff road. Then she turned a page and saw the picture of a man reading a newspaper. The newspaper was called the *Daily Bugle*. There were some words under the picture and Mia read them.

This is a picture of Larry Loop of the *Daily Bugle* news paper. He travelled round different towns, and readers of the *Daily Bugle* tried to find him. There was never a picture of him but he always carried a *Daily Bugle* news-paper. When readers guessed who he was, they said: 'You are Larry Loop and I want my £5 **prize**'. Several news-papers did this in the summer during the 1950s. This picture was taken in Crytchmoor Park on the 8th August,

1956, at eleven o'clock in the morning. It was taken just a few minutes before the terrible accident at Crytch Cove.

Mia closed the book. She didn't want to read any more about the accident. It was all too sad.

The shopkeeper was still busy with the customer. He waved when Mia and Jake went out of the shop.

'Did the other young visitors to Fig Cottage see the herring gull?' Mia asked Jake.

'Yes,' said Jake. 'I've talked to three of them in the last three years.'

'Did they go down to the beach?' said Mia.

'No,' said Jake. 'Only you and I have done that.'

'The herring gull seems to bring the past and today together,' said Mia. 'Like a Time Machine.'

'A Time Bird, you mean?' said Jake. 'Perhaps you're right.' He didn't seem interested any more. 'The fair's moving on to another town tomorrow, so I won't see you again,' he told Mia. 'I'm hoping we won't come back here next year. I don't want to see Crytch Cove again.'

Chapter Six

BACK IN TIME

Next morning, Mia was awake very early. She looked at the clock by her bed. It said 6.30. She got out of bed and went over to the window.

And she saw the herring gull.

'Fig!' she said.

Down the path Mia ran, the bird in front of her.

The bird was standing on the grass below her window. It seemed to be waiting for her.

Mia put on her T-shirt and some jeans, with her sun hat in the pocket, then went downstairs quietly. She didn't want to wake up her mother or Grandpa Morgan.

The herring gull waited until she was outside, then it flew towards the cliff path. Mia followed it . . .

. . . and it was like being part of the old brown photograph again. Down the path she ran, the bird in front of her. She heard the merry-go-round music before she reached the beach. This time, she walked on to the sand and stood among the people.

Mia was frightened. She heard the sound of her heart. What was going to happen now?

'Hallo,' a voice said.

A girl was standing in front of her. She was wearing a swimsuit, but it was not like Mia's swimsuit.

'Hallo,' Mia heard herself say. Her voice seemed to belong to another person.

The girl was looking at Mia's jeans and T-shirt. 'My name is Maureen Williams, and I'm fifteen,' she said. 'What's your name?'

'Mia,' Mia replied.

'Are you on holiday?' asked Maureen. Her voice sounded different. Then Mia realized this was because the girl came from Wales.

'Yes, I am,' answered Mia. 'We're staying at Fig Cottage.'

Mia looked at the newspaper. It was the Daily Bugle. She looked at the date on the top of the paper. 8th August, 1956.

'The cottage on the cliff road?' said Maureen. 'Is that a holiday cottage? I thought somebody was living there. There was a man working in the cottage garden yesterday.'

'Was there?' said Mia. Perhaps there was, she thought. What year is it?

She looked along the side of the cliff and saw a house. Or half a house. It was a large white building with a flat roof, but it wasn't finished. There was a big hole in front of the house.

For the swimming pool, thought Mia.

Maureen saw her looking at the house. 'Beautiful, isn't it?' she said. 'It must belong to a rich man.'

'It does,' said Mia.

'I like your sun hat,' said Maureen. 'I've never seen a sun hat like that. The rest of your clothes are strange, too.'

'What – what's the date?' Mia asked suddenly.

Maureen looked surprised. 'What an odd question,' she said. 'I'm not sure. I'll have to get Dad's newspaper.'

She walked over to a man and a woman who were sitting in deckchairs. There was a bag next to them and Maureen took a newspaper from it. She brought it back to Mia and gave it to her.

'8th August,' said Maureen.

Mia looked at the newspaper. It was the Daily Bugle. She looked at the date on the top of the paper. 8th August, 1956.

Chapter Seven

CAN I TAKE YOUR PICTURE?

'What's wrong?' Maureen asked.

'I – I don't . . .' Mia did not know how to explain. 'What's the time?' she asked.

Maureen looked at her watch. 'Half-past ten,' she said.

What time did the accident happen? thought Mia. She tried to remember. *Was it eleven o'clock in the morning? In half an hour?*

'I have to go,' she told Maureen. 'I can't stay here.'

'Are you afraid of something?' asked Maureen.

Mia did not answer for a minute. Then she said, 'You must not go on the merry-go-round.'

The other girl looked at Mia strangely. 'Why?' she said. 'I like going on the merry-go-round, it's exciting. I'm going on it again soon.'

'No!' Mia said. 'You can't! You mustn't! You must get away from here.'

'Get away from Crytch Cove?' said Maureen. 'Why?'

'Because it's dangerous here,' answered Mia. 'There's going to be an accident . . . today.'

'What accident?' said Maureen.

'The merry-go-round,' said Mia. 'It —'

'The merry-go-round?' said Maureen. 'An accident? How do you know?'

'I can't explain,' Mia told her. 'But you and your parents must get away from here.'

She was beginning to frighten the other girl. 'Who are you?' asked Maureen. 'Where are you from?'

'I — I'm from a long time away,' said Mia. 'Nearly forty years away. And I know what's going to happen here today.'

'You're stupid!' Maureen said. 'Give me back Dad's newspaper.'

Mia looked at the newspaper. She saw some words near the bottom of the front page.

LARRY LOOP IN CRYTCHMOOR TODAY. WIN £5!

Larry Loop!

38

Maureen saw her looking. 'Why do you want our newspaper?' she said suddenly. 'I know! You want it for Larry Loop. Where is he? Do you know?'

Mia remembered the picture in the book. A picture of Larry Loop in the park.

'Yes,' she said. 'Yes, I know.'

'Where?' asked Maureen.

Suddenly, Mia had an idea. 'I'll tell you,' she said. 'But you'll have to be quick. He won't be there long.'

'Where?' Maureen asked again.

'In the park, in Crytchmoor,' said Mia. 'Here's your newspaper. Now you can go and win five pounds.'

Maureen took the paper. 'I'm not sure,' she said. 'I don't really want to go to Crytchmoor. I want to stay here and swim in the sea. The beach is better here and I want another ride on the merry-go-round.'

'Please go!' said Mia. She saw the other girl looking at her sun hat. Mia pulled it off her head. 'You can have this, if you go,' she told Maureen.

'Your sun hat?' said Maureen. She smiled. 'Can I? Don't you want it?'

'You can have it if you go to Crytchmoor and win five pounds,' said Mia. 'But not if you don't.'

Maureen thought for a minute, then she said, 'All right, thanks.' And she took the hat and put it on her head. 'You're . . . strange,' she said.

'Yes, I know,' said Mia. 'Now go quickly.'

Maureen walked over to her parents. Mia watched her talking to them for a few minutes. They looked surprised, then they looked across at Mia.

Hurry! thought Mia.

Then Maureen and her parents began to pick up their things

from the beach. Mia watched them walk towards the cliff path. Maureen was wearing Mia's sun hat now, and she turned and waved. Mia waved back.

And then they were gone.

Now I must go, thought Mia. It must be nearly eleven o'clock.

'Can I take your picture?' said a voice.

Mia turned round and saw a man with a camera. 'I'm taking pictures for next year's Crytchmoor Tourist Book,' he said. 'Can I take a picture of you?'

Mia remembered the picture in the book. The book in the shop. 'No!' she said. 'I don't want my picture taken.'

'It'll only take a minute,' the man said. 'You can ride on the merry-go-round. I'll pay for the ride.'

'No!' Mia said again. 'I have to leave. I – I'm late.'

He was looking at Mia's clothes. 'Are you from America?' he said. 'Your clothes are strange.'

'No, I'm not,' said Mia. I have to get away, she thought. If he takes a picture of me, I'll be here for ever, I know I will. It'll be some other Mia going to stay at Fig Cottage forty years from now.

She began to run towards the cliff path. The man with the camera went across to the merry-go-round. Mia looked up at the white house on the cliff, then she looked at some children getting on the merry-go-round.

'Stop!' she shouted at them. But her voice sounded a long way away.

She wanted to run and stop them, but her feet were on the cliff path now.

And suddenly . . . Crytch Cove disappeared.

There was no merry-go-round, no cliffs, no beach, no sea. No people. Everything seemed to disappear into a white cloud. The cloud covered everything.

*Mia remembered the picture in the book . . . 'No!' she said. 'I
don't want my picture taken.'*

Mia became frightened. She could see nothing but white in front of her and behind her. She could not see the path, could not see her feet!

'Help!' she shouted.

Then she heard a sound. KYOW! KYOW!

'Fig!' she said. 'Where are you?'

KYOW! KYOW! The sound came from above and in front of her. Mia began to follow it through the white cloud. Slowly, the cloud began to get thinner . . .

. . . and then she saw the path and the bushes and the tall grass. She was at the top of the cliff, and there was the

Mia could see nothing but white in front of her and behind her. She could not see the path, could not see her feet!

sign. DANGER! KEEP OUT! There was Fig Cottage on the other side of the road.

Mia looked up in the sky to see the herring gull, with its yellow beak and grey wings. But it wasn't there. Suddenly, she knew something. It will never be there again, she thought. I've done the thing it wanted me to do, and now it's gone.

Chapter Eight

MAUREEN

Mia went to Crytchmoor with her mother and Grandpa Morgan that afternoon. She bought another sun hat, but there were no gulls on this one.

'Where's your other hat?' Mrs Dilon asked her.

'I – I lost it,' Mia said.

She did not want to tell her mother about Crytch Cove or about Maureen. Not yet. She won't believe me, thought Mia. She'll say I dreamed it. Or she'll be angry because I went down the cliff path. One day I'll tell her, but not now. We're on holiday and I don't want to make her angry.

They went to the beach again. Mia sat in a deckchair but then she remembered something. 'I think I'll walk into the town for half an hour,' she said. 'There's a book shop I want to visit.'

'Can I come with you?' asked Grandpa Morgan. 'I feel like a walk too.'

'OK,' said Mia.

They left Mrs Dilon on the beach, reading a book.

'Your mother's looking better,' said Grandpa Morgan.

'She works hard and this holiday was a good idea.'

'I know,' said Mia.

They walked through the narrow streets of the town. Crowds of people were going in and out of the little shops.

'Is anything wrong?' asked Grandpa Morgan, looking at Mia. 'You're very quiet today.'

'Am I?' said Mia. 'No, nothing's wrong.'

They found the book shop and went inside.

'Hallo,' said the shopkeeper, smiling at Mia. 'Back again?'

'I wanted to look at that book again,' said Mia. 'The one with the photographs.'

The shopkeeper found it for her. 'It's interesting, isn't it?' he said.

'Yes,' said Mia. She turned the pages, and saw her hands were shaking. She was looking for a picture, and at last she found the one she wanted to see again.

The faces of the people on the merry-go-round weren't very clear. Mia looked closely. She was sure Maureen wasn't one of them. Then she turned more pages and found the photograph of Larry Loop. There were some people walking along the path in the park. Walking towards Larry Loop. A man and a woman . . . and Maureen! And she was wearing a sun hat. *A sun hat with gulls on it.*

She escaped and got her prize! thought Mia. Maureen escaped, she wasn't killed. And it's because Fig took me back to help her.

Grandpa Morgan was watching her. 'You look pleased about something,' he said.

'I am,' said Mia.

'Is it that book?' said Grandpa Morgan. 'It does look interesting. Do you want it? I'll buy it for you. It can be a present.'

Mia put her arm round her grandfather and gave him a kiss. 'Thanks,' she said, smiling. 'That would be lovely.'

◆

Two days later, it was time to go home.

'We can stop at Mr Gurney's house and give him the key,' said Mrs Dilon, locking the door of Fig Cottage.

Mia was sad to be leaving the cottage. 'It was only a short holiday,' she said.

'But it was a good one,' said Grandpa Morgan.

'Yes, it was,' said Mrs Dilon.

They drove into Crytchmoor and found Mr and Mrs Gurney's house. Mr Gurney was working in the garden and there was a woman with him. She looked up when Mrs Dilon opened the car door.

'I brought the key for Fig Cottage,' said Mrs Dilon. 'We're going home now.'

The woman came across. 'Hallo,' she said. 'I'm Mrs Gurney. Have you enjoyed your holiday?'

Mia heard the woman's voice and thought, Did she once live in Wales? She speaks like somebody who once did. And then she remembered something. Maureen came from Wales. How strange.

'It was a lovely holiday,' Mrs Dilon was saying now. 'Crytchmoor is a nice place.'

'I used to come here when I was a girl,' said Mrs Gurney. 'We came here on holiday. Then I came to live here when Jack and I got married. We lived at Fig Cottage.'

'It was a comfortable cottage,' said Grandpa Morgan from the car. 'It's a pity you can't get down to the Cove.'

'I know,' said Mrs Gurney. 'Nobody likes to use it

45

because of the accident. But that was a long time ago now. Perhaps people will forget one day.'

'I was reading about the accident, yesterday,' said Mrs Dilon. 'In a book Mia bought.'

'Grandpa bought it,' said Mia. She looked at Mrs Gurney. 'Can I ask you a question?'

Mrs Gurney smiled. 'Yes, of course,' she said.

'Is your name . . . Maureen?' said Mia.

Mrs Gurney looked surprised. 'Yes, it is,' she said.

'I thought it was,' said Mia.

◆

They passed Fig Cottage again on their way out of the town. Mia didn't see the herring gull on the roof.

Not *the* herring gull.

EXERCISES

Vocabulary Work

Look back at the 'Dictionary Words' in this story. Do you know *all* the words?

1 Which are the words for:

   a living things?

   b parts of a bird's body?

   c things you can read?

   d something you can sit on?

   e a small house you can live in?

   f a thing you can win?

2 Look at the pictures and answer the questions.

   a *Page 6* What is standing on the roof of the cottage in this picture?

   b *Page 21* What is the man sitting on?

   c *Page 23* Where are Jake, Mia and her grandfather in this picture?

   d *Page 28* What can you see at the end of the beach, near the cliff?

   e *Page 41* What is the young boy making with the sand on the beach?

Comprehension

Chapters 1–2

1 Are the following sentences true (√) or not true (×)?

   a Mrs Dilon liked holidays.

   b Fig Cottage was on the cliff top.

   c Mia loved to watch birds.

   d Jake liked coming to Crytch Cove.

Chapters 3–4

2 Who said or thought these words?

   a 'You and your birds!'

   b '. . . I was only a child then.'

   c 'I had a bit too much sun yesterday, I think.'

Chapters 5–6

3 Look at this map of Crytch Cove.

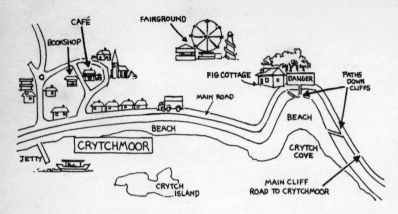

Where did the following things happen? Find them on the map.

a Mia and Jake had coffee here.

b Mia and Jake looked at the box of postcards here.

c Mia got out of bed and looked out of the window here.

Chapters 7–8

4 Find the answers to these questions.

a Why did Mia give Maureen her sunhat?

b Mia didn't want the man with the camera to take her picture. Why?

c Mia knew that Maureen wasn't killed in the accident? How?

Discussion

1 When strange things began to happen to Mia, she did not tell her mother about them. Was Mia right to keep quiet?

2 Would a time machine be a useful thing to have? Why or why not?

Writing

You are a newspaper reporter at the time the cliff fell down on the merry-go-round. Write a 200 word report of the accident for your newspaper.